Constellations

F. S. KIM

Children's Press®
A Division of Scholastic Inc.
New York Toronto London   Sydney
Mexico City New Delhi Hong Kong
Danbury, Connecticut

Content Consultant

Noreen Grice

Astronomer

President, You Can Do Astronomy, LLC.

www.youcandoastronomy.com

Library of Congress Cataloging-in-Publication Data

Kim, F. S.
  Constellations / by F. S. Kim.
      p. cm.—(A true book)
  Includes index.
    ISBN-13: 978-0-531-16895-0 (lib. bdg.)   978-0-531-22802-9 (pbk.)
    ISBN-10: 0-531-16895-6 (lib. bdg.)   0-531-22802-9 (pbk.)

1. Constellations—Juvenile literature. I. Title. II. Series.

QB802.K53 2010
523.8—dc22   2008050629

1 2 3 4 5 6 7 8 9 10 R 19 18 17 16 15 14 13 12 11 10   62

Find the Truth!

Everything you are about to read is true *except* for one of the sentences on this page.

Which one is **TRUE**?

T or F   The stars in a constellation are near each other in space.

T or F   The Big Dipper is not an official constellation. It's an asterism.

Find the answers in this book.

Contents

Zodiac Wheel

Taurus was one of the first constellations to be named.

THE **BIG** TRUTH!

Asterisms

5 Constellations Around the World

From a dark location, far away from city lights, you can see thousands of stars without a telescope.

CHAPTER 1

The Stars in Our Sky

The stars in the sky are grouped into 88 constellations.

On a clear night, when you are away from city lights, you might see lots of stars. If you have ever imagined connecting the stars to make pictures, you're not alone. People have been doing this for thousands of years. The stars that form some of these imaginary pictures are called **constellations**.

Helpful Stars

Stars and constellations have helped people since ancient times. Before there were clocks or calendars, people used the Sun, Moon, and stars to help them tell time. They also used stars to find their way when they were lost at night. The histories of ancient people have been passed along in stories about constellations.

Explorers of the past crossed the Pacific Ocean guided by the stars.

Today, astronauts use Canopus to help them find their way.

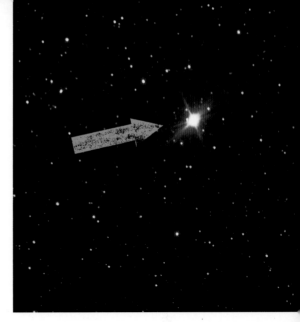

Canopus is the second-brightest star in the sky. It helped to guide sailors in the Mediterranean for many centuries.

Today, people don't rely on the stars to tell time or get directions. But constellations are still very important. Constellations remind us about stories that were created long ago. And the pictures and patterns that people have been seeing for so many years help us keep in mind the stars that shine brightly above us.

CHAPTER 2

The View From Earth

Most stars in the universe are one to ten billion years old.

Stars are large glowing balls of gas. However, they look very small to us in the night sky because they are actually far away. Our view of the stars depends on where we are on Earth and the location of Earth in its annual trip around the Sun.

The Big Dipper

Farther from Earth

Closer to Earth

Not as They Appear

The stars in constellations look like they are near each other in space and the same distance from Earth. But that's not always true. Stars in constellations can be different distances from Earth.

The two stars in the picture of the Big Dipper look like they are the same distance from Earth. However, one star is actually much closer to Earth than the other star.

Spinning in Circles

If you stand outside at different times during the night, you'll see the stars have moved across the sky. But the stars aren't really moving. It's actually you. Earth is **rotating** or spinning like a giant slowly-moving merry-go-round in space. When you ride a merry-go-round, it seems like the people waiting in line are turning around you. But it's really you that is moving! The stars are like the people standing in line.

North and South

Your location on Earth affects how you see constellations. Earth can be divided into halves called hemispheres. The **Northern Hemisphere** is the half north of the equator. People here can see the North Star and constellations around it. To see many southern stars, you would need to be south of the equator, in the **Southern Hemisphere**. The closer you are to the North Pole, the more northern stars you can see. The closer you are to the South Pole, the more southern stars you can see.

North Pole

Equator

South Pole

The equator is the imaginary line around the center of Earth.

At the equator, Earth spins faster than 1,000 miles (1,609 kilometers) per hour.

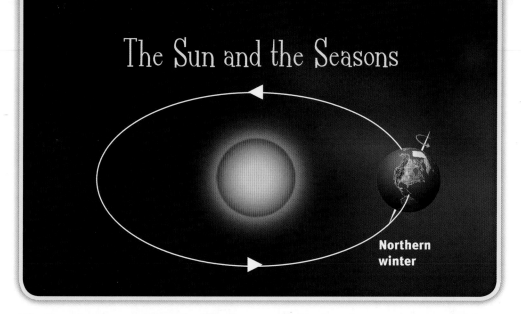

The Sun and the Seasons

Northern winter

The hemisphere of Earth tilted toward the Sun has summer and the hemisphere tilted away has winter. Because only one pole can face the Sun at a time, the Northern and Southern Hemispheres have opposite seasons.

Travels Through Space

You might notice that the stars on a winter night seem different than the ones you see in summer. That's true. As Earth spins, it also travels around the Sun in an **orbit**. The stars that we see after sunset in the summer aren't the same ones we see after sunset in the winter. This is because our view of the stars changes as Earth orbits the Sun.

15

The ancient Babylonians, Chinese, and Egyptians were among the first to record the movements of the stars and planets.

CHAPTER 3

A History of Constellations

Astronomy is the study of space and everything in it. It is the oldest of all the different kinds of sciences. Thousands of years ago, people believed that the stars and planets were controlled by gods. Early astronomers believed that they could instead use science to explain why these objects moved and changed their positions in the sky.

The word astronomy comes from the ancient Greek words astro, or star, and *nomia*, or law.

More than 3,000 years ago, the Babylonians recorded the movements of the stars on clay tablets like this one.

Ancient Civilizations

Stars were important to early civilizations. People living during these times didn't have clocks or calendars. Instead, they studied the stars to keep track of time and the seasons. When a certain bright star rose before the Sun, the ancient Egyptians knew it was flood season for the Nile River. The ancient Babylonians grouped stars into constellations and even made a calendar.

Much of what we know about early astronomy comes from the ancient Greeks. The most famous Greek astronomer is Ptolemy (TAHL-oh-mee). Ptolemy lived in Egypt during the 2nd century. In about 150 C.E., he put together a book called

Ptolemy claimed that Earth was the center of the universe. Even though he was wrong, people believed this to be true for nearly 1,500 years.

the *Almagest* (AL-muh-jest) that included the known constellations and his beliefs about the motions of the stars, planets, Sun, and Moon.

The name *Almagest* comes from the Arabic *al-majisti* and means "the greatest."

Stonehenge

Stonehenge is a prehistoric monument in Wiltshire, England. Some parts of this circle of large stones and earth mounds date back to around 2,800 B.C.E. The biggest stones weigh up to 50 tons (45 metric tons). Some scientists believe that Stonehenge was used by ancient people as a calendar to track the positions of the Sun, Moon, and stars.

Early astronomers used many tools like these to study the stars.

Astrolabe

Armillary sphere

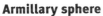

Sextant

Quadrant

Follow That Star

Ptolemy wrote about 48 constellations but there were actually many more that would be found. Once people began building ships to explore the world and trade goods with far-off countries, they looked to the skies, too. Back then, sailors would find their way at sea during the night by using tools to observe the stars. As astronomers discovered new groups of stars, they named new constellations to go with them.

Keeping Constellations Organized

The telescope was invented in the 1600s. This new tool helped astronomers see more stars than ever before. Astronomers began including these newly discovered stars in the constellations they had already been studying. But they didn't all agree on how these stars should be grouped. Eventually, many stars were listed in more than one constellation and this caused confusion.

Constellation Timeline

150 C.E.
Ptolemy publishes *Almagest*. It contains 48 constellations.

1596
Dutch sailors begin mapping stars in the Southern Hemisphere.

In 1930, astronomers decided to organize the way constellations were grouped. The International Astronomical Union (IAU) is a group of professional astronomers. It made an official list of 88 constellations. On this list, which is still in use today, each star could not be part of more than one constellation. The night sky was also divided into 88 sections—one for each constellation.

1930

The International Astronomical Union makes an official list of 88 constellations.

1687
Johannes Hevelius invents seven new constellations.

Many years ago, astronomers made maps of the stars and used pictures to show the constellations. This map of the Southern Hemisphere is from 1725.

CHAPTER 4

Star Stories

For as long as people have viewed stars in the sky, they have invented stories about them. The names for many constellations come from Greek stories or **myths**. These myths often explained how stars first got to where they are. They celebrated gods and heroes. Today, constellations remind us of these ancient stories.

Constellations include pictures of people, animals, and objects.

Ursa Major

Ursa Major, also known as the Great Bear, is a constellation in the Northern Hemisphere. The Big Dipper is a star pattern within the constellation of Ursa Major, or the Great Bear. There are many stories behind Ursa Major. According to one, the Greek goddess Hera was jealous of a woman named Callisto and turned Callisto into a bear. The god Zeus swept Callisto into the sky before she could be killed by a hunter.

Ursa Major is in the Northern Hemisphere. It's the third largest constellation.

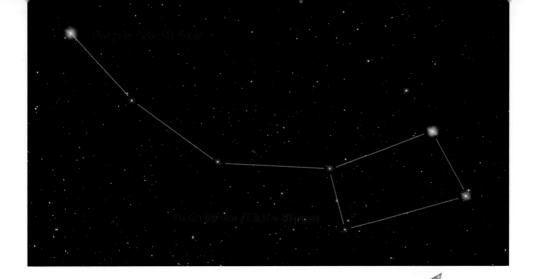

Some myths say that Callisto's son, Arcas, was turned into Ursa Minor.

Ursa Minor

The Little Dipper is a star pattern within the constellation of Ursa Minor. Ursa Minor is also called the Little Bear. The North Star, Polaris, is located at the very end of the handle of the Little Dipper. Polaris sits right above the North Pole so it appears not to move. For thousands of years, people have used this star to find their way north.

Orion

The constellation Orion (or-RYE-un) can be seen in the Northern and Southern Hemispheres. Orion's belt is made up of a row of three stars. The bright stars Betelgeuse (BET-el-jooze) and Rigel (RYE-jel) form Orion's shoulder and foot. There are many different Greek myths about Orion. According to one, the goddess Artemis fell in love with Orion. When he was accidentally killed, Artemis placed his body among the stars.

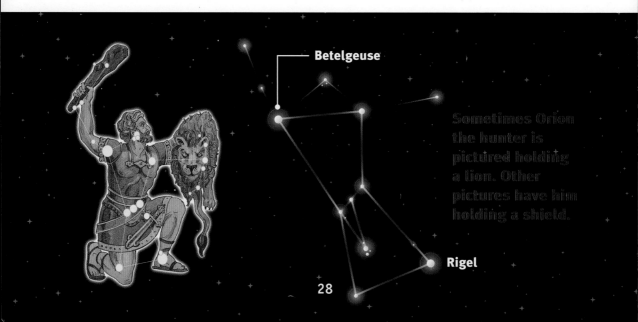

Betelgeuse

Sometimes Orion the hunter is pictured holding a lion. Other pictures have him holding a shield.

Rigel

28

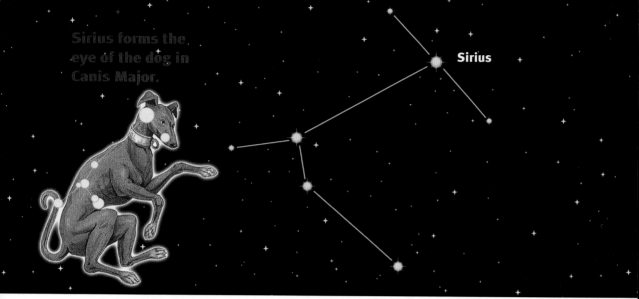

Sirius forms the eye of the dog in Canis Major.

Sirius

The star Sirius is more than 20 times brighter than the Sun.

Canis Major

When Orion was sent into the sky, some Greek legends say that his hunting dogs came along, too. Canis Major is also called the Great Dog. It contains Sirius, the brightest star in the night sky. Sirius looks bright because it's one of the closest stars to Earth. This constellation can be seen both in the Northern and Southern Hemispheres.

Cassiopeia

On a clear night in the Northern Hemisphere, Cassiopeia (CASS-ee-oh-PEE-ah) is easy to spot. It looks like a W, as well as a crown. In Greek myths, Cassiopeia was a proud queen who thought she was very beautiful. Her pride angered the sea god Poseidon (puh-SYE-don). As punishment, she sits on her throne in the sky and during some parts of the year, she looks like she's hanging upside-down.

Many people in the ancient Middle East thought Cassiopeia looked like a kneeling camel.

Crux

Crux is the smallest constellation and the most famous in the Southern Hemisphere. It is also called the Southern Cross because of its shape. Crux helped guide early sailors because the long part of the cross points south. This constellation also has a large dark patch called the *Coalsack*. The Coalsack is a big cloud of gas and dust called a **nebula**.

The Southern Cross appears on the flags of several countries including Australia and New Zealand.

The Coalsack

New Zealand flag

Scorpius

Scorpius (SKOR-pee-uhss) is one of the few constellations that looks like the animal it's named after—a scorpion. You could say that Scorpius looks like a giant J, too. Scorpius can be seen in both the Northern and Southern Hemispheres. It's found in the summer sky while Orion is in the winter sky. According to one Greek myth, the hunter Orion boasted that he could kill any wild animal. It is said that the goddess who protected Earth was angered by Orion's pride so she sent a scorpion to sting him.

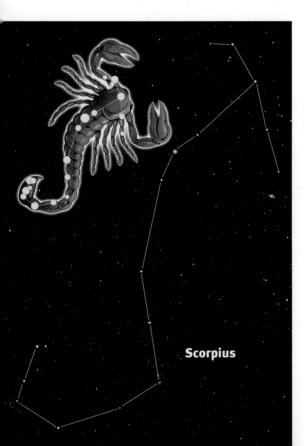

Scorpius

Hercules

Hercules (HER-cue-leez) is the Roman name for the ancient Greek hero, Heracles. Greek myths say that Heracles was the half-human son of the god Zeus. Heracles was very strong and very smart. His greatest acts included killing the Hydra, a monster with nine heads. To honor him, Zeus placed Heracles among the stars. The constellation Hercules can be viewed in both the Northern and Southern Hemispheres.

One of the longest constellations in the sky is named Hydra, after a monster that Hercules defeated.

Hercules

Asterisms

The Big Dipper and the Little Dipper are called asterisms. Asterisms are stars that people have grouped together, but they aren't official constellations. Sometimes asterisms are part of one constellation. Sometimes one or two stars from several different constellations make up an asterism.

Teapot

Many people see a teapot in the constellation of Sagittarius.

Kite

The constellation of Boötes (boh-OH-teez) is sometimes called the kite. You can see an ice cream cone in this constellation, too.

Butterfly

If lines are drawn to connect the arms and legs on the left and right of Hercules, you can see a butterfly.

The Sickle

The head of the constellation Leo is sometimes called the sickle. A sickle is a farming tool. Today, Leo's head reminds people of a backwards question mark.

Chinese sky watchers grouped the sky into four sections.
The sections were named after four creatures—a dragon,
a bird, a white tiger, and a black tortoise.

CHAPTER 5

Constellations Around the World

When different people view the same object, they don't always have the same thoughts about what they see. This is true for constellations, too. Most stories about the official constellations come from ancient Greece and Europe. Other cultures have explained the stars in their own ways. They have looked to animals and stories from their parts of the world to help draw patterns and pictures in the sky.

A Different View

The stars that make up the constellation Leo reminded European astronomers of a lion. To the ancient Chinese, Leo looked like a horse. The Lakota, a Native American tribe, saw the bottom half of Orion as a hand. The Chinook tribe saw Orion's belt and sword as two canoes in a race.

However, sometimes different cultures saw almost the same thing in the sky. The ancient Syrians agreed with the Greeks about Orion. They saw a person in the sky. The Syrians called Orion *Al Jabbar*, which means "the Giant". In the constellation Ursa Major, the Iroquois tribe also saw a bear. But they didn't give Ursa Major a long tail like the Greeks did. Instead, they saw these stars as hunters. The hunters chased the bear across the sky from spring until the fall.

The Sioux Indians of North America thought the Big Dipper looked like a skunk.

Gods and the Stars

Still other people saw religious meanings in the stars. Many civilizations around the world thought that stars were gods. The constellation of Scorpius is very important to the Maori (MAU-ree) tribe of New Zealand. They believe that the god Maui used this constellation as a fishhook. In their constellation story, Maui pulled up one of the islands of New Zealand from the ocean's bottom using Scorpius.

The fishhook is an important symbol in Maori culture. It is used in carvings, jewelry, and paintings.

Astrology

Astrology is the belief that the position of the Sun, Moon, and planets affect a person's personality and life. Western astrology uses the **zodiac**, which is made up of 12 constellations. From Earth, the Sun, Moon, and planets appear to move through these constellations during the year. **Astrologers** look at the position of the planets and stars on a person's birth date. They believe that this will tell them about a person's future.

The word zodiac comes from the Greek word *zodiackos* or "circle of animals."

Lessons in the Stars

Through the study of constellations, we've learned stories of people that lived long ago. And today's astronomers are lucky enough to be able to study the same sky that these ancient people observed for thousands of years before us. Now we know much more about the universe around us as well as the science behind the stars. Constellations help everyone learn their way around the night sky. ★

True Statistics

Number of stars that can be viewed without a telescope: A few thousand

Number of stars in the Milky Way: About 400 billion

Number of constellations: 88

Constellations in the zodiac: Aries, Taurus, Gemini, Cancer, Leo, Virgo, Libra, Scorpius, Sagittarius, Capricornus, Aquarius, and Pisces

Closest star to Earth: Proxima Centauri

Largest constellation: Hydra

Smallest constellation: Crux

Did you find the truth?

F The stars in a constellation are near each other in space.

T The Big Dipper is not an official constellation. It's an asterism.

Resources

Books

Levy, David H. *Skywatching*. Alexandria, VA: Time-Life Books, 1994.

Lippincott, Kristen. *Astronomy* (Eyewitness Science). New York: DK Publishing, 2004.

Mechler, Gary. *The National Audubon Society First Field Guide: Night Sky*. New York: Scholastic, 1999.

Mitton, Jacqueline, and Simon Mitton. *Scholastic Encyclopedia of Space*. New York: Scholastic, 1999.

Sasaki, Chris. *Constellations: A Glow-in-the-Dark Guide to the Night Sky*. New York: Sterling Publishing, 2006.

Wright, Kenneth. *Scholastic Atlas of Space*. New York: Scholastic, 2005.

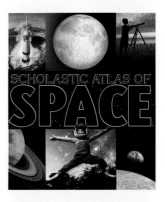

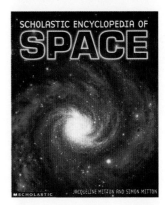

Organizations and Web Sites

AstroViewer
www.astroviewer.com
Use the online interactive sky map to see the constellations in your area.

International Astronomical Union
www.iau.org/public_press/themes/constellations/
Look at the official star charts for all 88 constellations.

Windows to the Universe
www.windows.ucar.edu
Learn more about the mythology of the constellations at this site.

Places to Visit

Adler Planetarium
1300 South Lake Shore Drive
Chicago, IL 60605
(312) 922 7827
www.adlerplanetarium.org
Learn how ancient people used stars to tell time, navigate their way and more.

Clark Planetarium
110 South 400 West
Salt Lake City, UT 84101
(801) 456 7827
www.clarkplanetarium.org
Learn how a telescope works and see proof that the Earth actually rotates.

Important Words

astrologers – people who practice astrology

astrology – the study of how the position of the planets and stars may affect people's lives

astronomy – the study of space and everything in it

constellations – group of stars that seem to make a pattern in the sky. Astronomers divide the sky into 88 constellations.

myths – stories that express the beliefs of a group of people

nebula – a giant cloud of gas and dust in space

Northern Hemisphere – the half of Earth that is north of the equator

orbit – the path of a planet or other object around the Sun

rotating – spinning in space

Southern Hemisphere – the half of Earth that is south of the equator

zodiac – an area of the sky that includes 12 constellations and the path of the Sun, Moon, and planets

Index

Page numbers in **bold** indicate illustrations

About the Author

F. S. Kim has been writing and editing children's books since 2002. Her many projects include extreme animals, dinosaurs, ocean life, survival guides, crafts, and much more. Ms. Kim first became interested in constellations at Vassar College during an astronomy class. When she's not working on books, Ms. Kim looks for stars over her backyard in New York City.